FALL
BACK-TO-SCHOOL
BADGE
BOOK

How To Use This Book

Your Badge Book connects you to two reading challenges this fall: one for September and one for November. (Don't worry, we've got plenty of activities lined up to keep you reading in October and December too!)

If your school or library offers the Fall Badge Book Program:

1 Have your parent, librarian, or teacher log you in to the Beanstack app or Beanbright for Schools.

2 Join the 'Fall Badge Book Challenge.'

3 Keep track of what, when, and how much you read by logging in the app.

4 Earn Badges online that match with the stickers in the book. Place the stickers in the right spots and do the activities.

If you do not have a library or school offering the Fall Badge Book:

Visit badgebook.com/getstarted for more instructions. It only takes a minute or two to be up and reading!

READY? LET'S GO! ➜

Draw Yourself Here

This is _____ 's Book

READING PLEDGE

⭐ I am _____ years old.

⭐ I am in the _____ grade.

⭐ My hometown is _____

_____.

⭐ I like books about _____

_____.

**I hereby pledge to read books that I love,
all autumn long!**

OFFICIAL SIGNATURE

FALL
Reading Challenge I

BACK-TO-SCHOOL

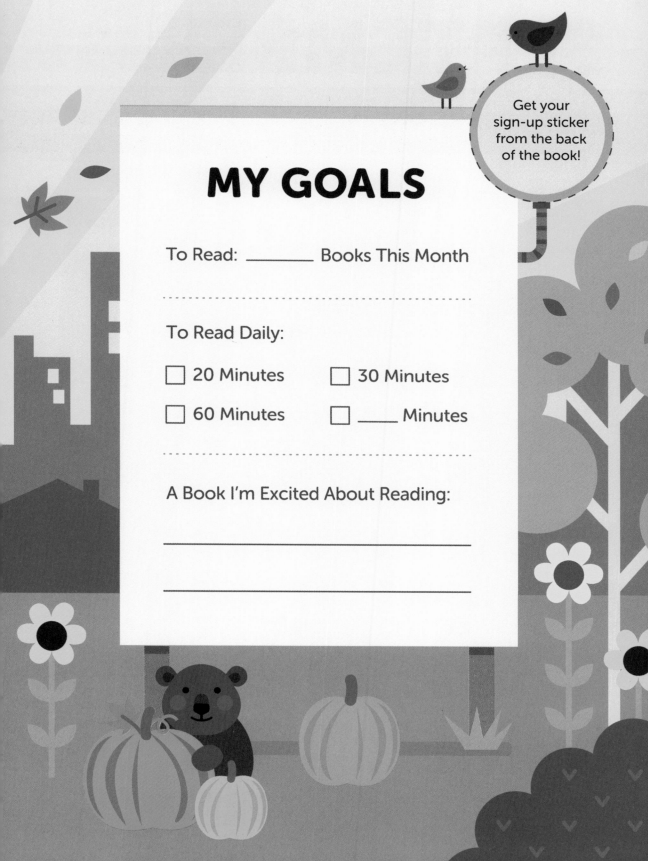

MY GOALS

Get your sign-up sticker from the back of the book!

To Read: _____ Books This Month

To Read Daily:

☐ 20 Minutes   ☐ 30 Minutes

☐ 60 Minutes   ☐ _____ Minutes

A Book I'm Excited About Reading:

_____

_____

SEPTEMBER

SUNDAY	MONDAY	TUESDAY	WEDNESDAY
		1	**2**
6 Read a Book Day	**7**	**8** International Literacy Day	**9**
13 Roald Dahl Day	**14**	**15** National Hispanic Heritage Month Begins	**16**
20	**21**	**22** Dear Diary Day — Hobbit Day	**23**
27 Banned Books Week	**28**	**29**	**30**

Every time you read, peel a daily-reader sticker, and stick it in your calendar to mark the day!

THURSDAY	FRIDAY	SATURDAY	
3	4	5	
10	11	12	
17	18	19	
24	25	26	

Way to go!
Put your
sticker here.

Splendid!
Put your
sticker here.

Put 'er there!
Put your
sticker here.

REMEMBER: Log reading through Beanstack or Beanbright to unlock the stickers and find out which ones go on this page!

Have fun filling in this storytime mad lib!

The Merry Adventures of Robin

_____
[an article of clothing]

In _____ England in times of old, lived the outlaw
[adjective (a describing word)]

Robin and his friends: _____ John, Friar
[adjective (a describing word)]

_____, and _____ Marian. Now, verily did
[name for a pet]   [a job]

the Sheriff of _____-Ham hate Robin's gang,
[verb (an action word) ending in "ing"]

for they stole _____ from the rich, and gave them to the
[plural noun (things)]

poor—who always thanked them with a hearty "_____!"
[a silly nonsense word]

and gave them plenty of cold _____ to eat in return.
[a food]

So the Sheriff announced a competition. "Hear ye!

Whosoever shooteth best with a _____ shall win
[a kitchen tool]

the Golden _____." Bold Robin came in disguise, dyeing
[noun (a thing)]

his beard _____ and wearing a patch over his
[a color]

_____, but when his final shot split the target in
[a part of the body]

_____ pieces, the Sheriff leapt up. "'Tis Robin!" quoth he.
[a number]

"Seize that saucy_____!" Luckily, clever Marian
[an insulting name to call someone]

tripped the Sheriff, who fell face down in the _____, and
[something mushy]

the outlaws hopped on their trusty _____ and rode to
[an animal (plural)]

freedom, shouting "Long live the true King, _____!"
[a famous person]

You got moxie, kid! Put your sticker here.

Stick it to me! Put your sticker here.

You da champ! Put your sticker here.

REMEMBER: Log reading through Beanstack or Beanbright to unlock the stickers and find out which ones go on this page!

Create your own story out of some
surprise ingredients.
Tell it out loud to a friend!

boy, girl, scientist,
piglet, scout, dragon,
detective

desert, empty school,
Hawaii, party, cave,
Atlantis

A _____ traveled to a _____

and met a _____ who was _____.

The story also has a _____!

robot, python,
grandmother, chef, pixie,
guitarist, pilot

crying, super fast,
hungry, whispering, lost,
celebrating, enchanted

fountain, chocolate,
tornado, song,
roller skates, tiny sword

Give your story a title!

Read About:
HISPANIC HERITAGE

September is National Hispanic Heritage Month, honoring the contributions of Hispanic and Latinx Americans to our country's history and culture. Hispanic heritage includes people whose ancestors are from Spain, Mexico, the Caribbean, Central America, or South America, so it's a big group—the second-largest in America, with more than 60,000,000 members!

You can read all kinds of books for Hispanic Heritage Month: descriptions of life in Latin countries, biographies of famous people, stories about family traditions, poetry in two languages, novels about Hispanic characters, and more.

Here are a few great titles—ask your librarian about others!

1. ***Dalia's Wondrous Hair / El cabello maravilloso de Dalia*** by Laura Lacámara: A Cuban girl turns her amazing hair into a tower filled with nature. (Ages 4+)

2. ***Funny Bones: Posada and His Day of the Dead Calaveras*** by Duncan Tonatiuh: The true story of the Mexican artist who drew Day of the Dead skeletons (like the ones from the movie Coco). (Ages 6+)

3. ***The First Rule of Punk*** by Celia C. Pérez: Even though her mother disapproves, Malú starts her own band because she needs to rock. (Ages 9+)

You got moxie, kid!
Put your
sticker here.

Stick it to me!
Put your
sticker here.

You da champ!
Put your
sticker here.

REMEMBER: Log reading through Beanstack or Beanbright to unlock the stickers and find out which ones go on this page!

DRAWING TIME

The pictures on flags always have meaning.
The Mexican eagle stands for the Aztec empire,
while the Nicaraguan flag shows a cap symbolizing
freedom and a rainbow for a bright future.

If you started your own country, what would you draw on
your flag? Make it colorful enough to see from far away!

You're a reading machine! Put your sticker here.

Stupendous achievement! Put your sticker here.

You go, power reader! Put your sticker here.

REMEMBER: Log reading through Beanstack or Beanbright to unlock the stickers and find out which ones go on this page!

You're a detective! Time to do some research on a "suspect." Choose an **author** or **illustrator** you like, and look them up online. Can you fill out the clues below?

Name:

- -

Where they live:

- -

Book title you haven't read yet:

- -

One interesting detail about them:

- -

- -

✳ **BONUS:** write them an email or letter and tell them what you like about their book!

SEPTEMBER HIGHLIGHTS AND FAVORITES!

📖 Book I Want to Read Again: _____

_____

💬 Hot New Word: _____

_____

👍 Bravest Character: _____

_____

🎨 Book With the Most Interesting Illustrations:

_____

_____

🗺 Most Unusual Place I Read a Book: _____

_____

JUST FOR FUN!

Read a book in the tub (carefully!).

Check the Beanstack App to Fill In These Stats:

Longest Book Read:

Number of Reading Sessions:

Most Pages in a Session:

Total Books Read:

Wow! That much reading already?
Fill in some more about what you read and how you did!

One fact you learned about nature or history:

What's your favorite part of the library?

YAHOO! You just completed this season's Reading Challenge. That's some serious brain exercise!

— CERTIFICATE OF —
COMPLETION

Get your sticker from the back of the book!

AWARDED TO:

Name: _____

Date: _____

Number of Badges Earned: _____

Signature: _____

You don't have to wait for the next Challenge to continue—keep on reading! You can keep track of your accomplishments on the next pages.

OCTOBER

SUNDAY	MONDAY	TUESDAY	WEDNESDAY
4	5	6	7
11 Teen Read Week	12	13	14
18	19	20	21
25	26	27	28

THURSDAY	FRIDAY	SATURDAY	
1 National Book Month — Star Wars Reads Day	2	3	
8	9	10	
15	16 Dictionary Day	17	
22	23	24	
29	30	31	

Read Some:

SCIENCE FICTION

Science Fiction (or "sci-fi") tells stories about what might happen to people in the future. It often describes technology that doesn't exist yet, like spaceships to other planets, computers that think for themselves, or medicines that keep people alive forever. Some sci-fi writers imagine Earth thousands of years from now, while others write about life "tomorrow."

You probably know some science-fiction already! The genre includes everything from famous books like *Frankenstein* and *20,000 Leagues Under the Sea* (written almost 200 years ago) to modern stories like *WALL-E* and *Star Wars*.

Here are some more sci-fi titles you can check out as well. Ask your librarian about others!

1. *Oh, No! (Or How My Science Project Destroyed The World)* by Mac Barnett: A young inventor builds a robot with laser eyes and unstoppable super claws. (Ages 5+)

2. *Hello, Nebulon!* by Ray O'Ryan: In the year 2120, Jack moves to a new school—on a new planet. (Ages 6+)

3. *The City of Ember* by Jeanne DuPrau: When the lights start to go out in the last human city, it's up to two kids to solve the mystery before everything goes dark. (Ages 8+)

My Life
IN THE YEAR
2040

Twenty years in the future, what will you be up to?

I'll live in:

My job will be:

Everyone will eat:

I will drive a:

People's most useful tool will be:

OCTOBER HIGHLIGHTS
AND FAVORITES!

📖 Book I'd Recommend to My Friends: _____

_____

🌐 A New Place I Read About: _____

_____

😝 Silliest Character: _____

_____

📕 Best Book Cover: _____

_____

🧑‍🏫 Someone Who Read to Me (or With Me): _____

_____

_____

⚡ JUST FOR FUN! ⚡

**Read a story out loud to someone
younger than you!**

Check the Beanstack App to Fill In These Stats:

Longest Book Read:

Number of Reading Sessions:

Most Pages in a Session:

Total Books Read:

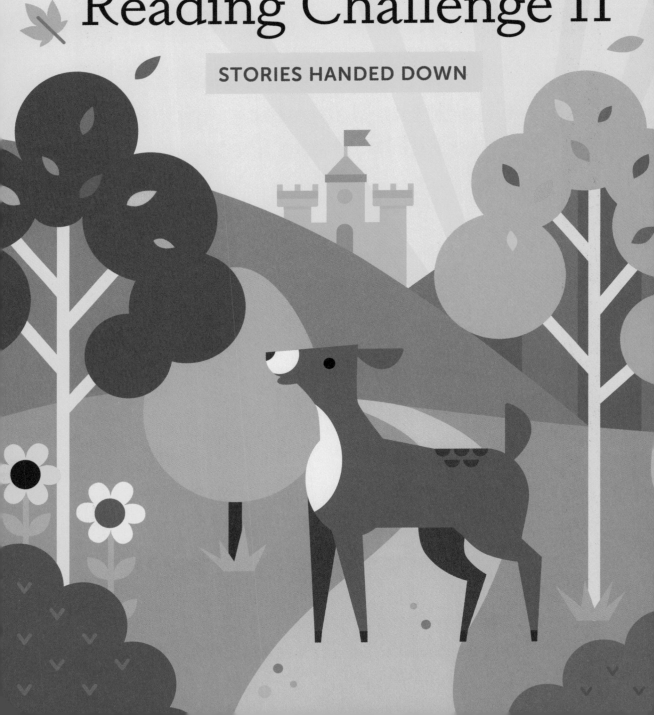

FALL
Reading Challenge II

STORIES HANDED DOWN

Get your sign-up sticker from the back of the book!

MY GOALS

To Read: ———— Books This Month

To Read Daily:

☐ 20 Minutes   ☐ 30 Minutes

☐ 60 Minutes   ☐ ____ Minutes

A Book I'm Excited About Reading:

_____

_____

NOVEMBER

SUNDAY	MONDAY	TUESDAY	WEDNESDAY
1 Picture Book Month — Family Literacy Month — Native American Heritage Month	**2**	**3**	**4**
8	**9**	**10**	**11**
15 I Love to Write Day	**16**	**17**	**18** High-Five a Librarian Day
22	**23**	**24**	**25**
29	**30** Mark Twain's Birthday		

Every time you read, peel a daily-reader sticker, and stick it in your calendar to mark the day!

THURSDAY	FRIDAY	SATURDAY
5 National Non-Fiction Day	6	7
12	13	14
19	20	21
26	27	28

You're a reading machine! Put your sticker here.

Stupendous achievement! Put your sticker here.

You go, power reader! Put your sticker here.

REMEMBER: Log reading through Beanstack or Beanbright to unlock the stickers and find out which ones go on this page!

Look into your crystal ball—
write or draw what happens next in
the story you just read!

You got moxie, kid!
Put your
sticker here.

Stick it to me!
Put your
sticker here.

You da champ!
Put your
sticker here.

REMEMBER: Log reading through Beanstack or Beanbright to unlock the stickers and find out which ones go on this page!

What magic potion could have been really helpful in one of the books you just read? Write a recipe for it here:

NAME OF POTION:

_____

_____

RECIPE:

_____

_____

_____

_____

_____

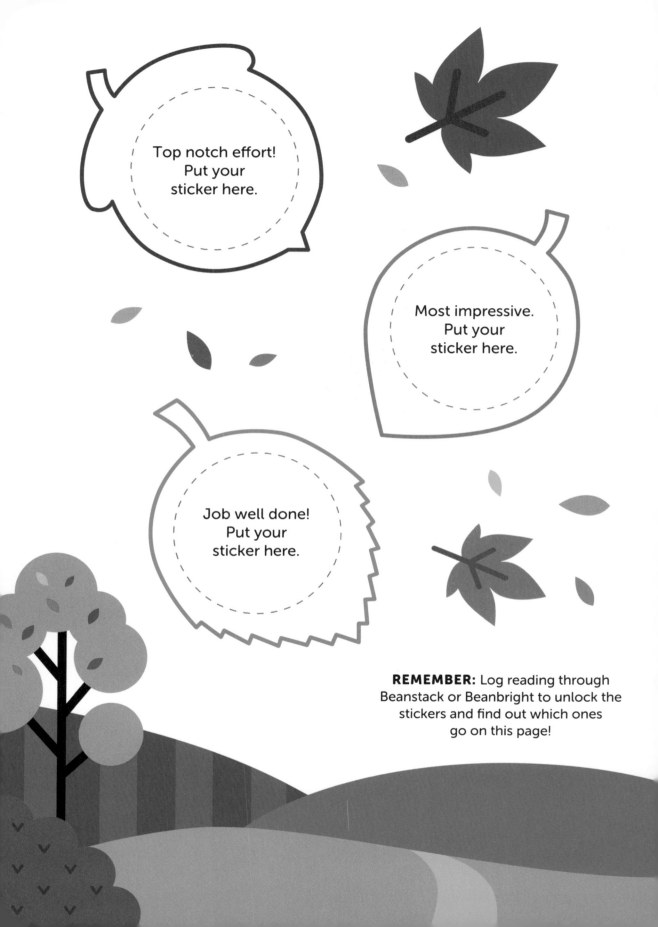

Top notch effort!
Put your
sticker here.

Most impressive.
Put your
sticker here.

Job well done!
Put your
sticker here.

REMEMBER: Log reading through Beanstack or Beanbright to unlock the stickers and find out which ones go on this page!

Design your perfect clubhouse! What will the building look like? Draw the cool stuff you will put inside each room.

1	NAME OF ARCHITECT:
2	WHERE WILL IT BE LOCATED?:
3	COST TO BUILD:

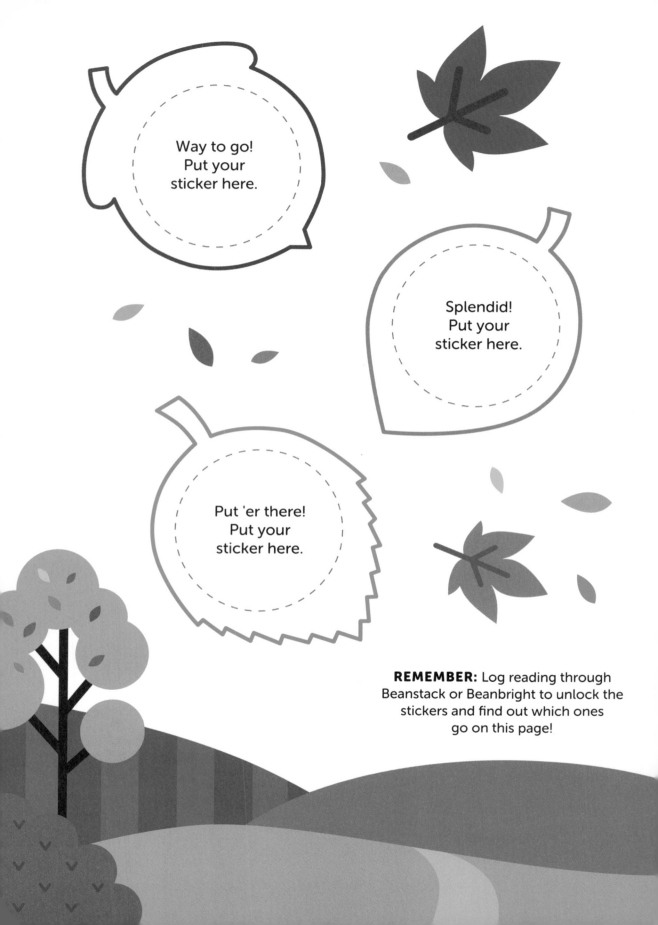

Way to go!
Put your
sticker here.

Splendid!
Put your
sticker here.

Put 'er there!
Put your
sticker here.

REMEMBER: Log reading through Beanstack or Beanbright to unlock the stickers and find out which ones go on this page!

Make a hero card for one of the characters you like best!

Name:

Draw their portrait here:

Age: _____

Location: _____

Special Skill: _____

Favorite Snack: _____

Best Friend: _____

NOVEMBER HIGHLIGHTS
AND FAVORITES!

📖 Book I Want to Read Again: _____

_____

💬 Hot New Word: _____

_____

👍 Bravest Character: _____

_____

🎨 Book With the Most Interesting Illustrations:

_____

_____

🗺️ Most Unusual Place I Read a Book: _____

_____

JUST FOR FUN!

Read a book in the tub (carefully!).

Check the Beanstack App to Fill In These Stats:

Longest Book Read:

Number of Reading Sessions:

Most Pages in a Session:

Total Books Read:

Wow! That much reading already?
Fill in some more about what you read and how you did!

One interesting place you read about:

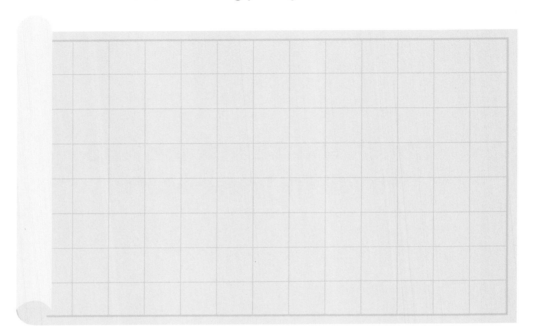

Draw your favorite heroine.

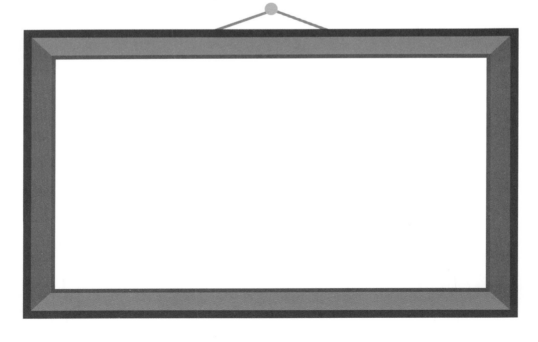

YAHOO! You just completed this season's Reading Challenge. That's some serious brain exercise!

— CERTIFICATE OF —
COMPLETION

Get your sticker from the back of the book!

AWARDED TO:

Name: _____

Date: _____

Number of Badges Earned: _____

Signature: _____

You don't have to wait for the next Challenge to continue—keep on reading!
You can keep track of your accomplishments on the next pages.

DECEMBER

SUNDAY	MONDAY	TUESDAY	WEDNESDAY
		1	2
6	7	8	9
13	14	15	16 Jane Austen's Birthday
20	21	22	23
27	28	29	30

Every time you read, peel a daily-reader sticker, and stick it in your calendar to mark the day!

THURSDAY	FRIDAY	SATURDAY	
3	4	5	
10	11	12	
17	18	19	
24	25	26	
31			

Read A:
BOOK OF POEMS

Some poems rhyme, and some don't. Some follow strict rules, and some—called "free verse"—can just sound like someone talking. There are short 3-line poems, like haiku, and there are "epic" poems so long they fill whole books. There are poems about flowers and feelings, and poems about sword battles and Cyclops.

So what makes a poem? Usually, poets pay close attention to the **rhythm** of their words—how they sound when read aloud. Poets also choose each word carefully, looking for strong meanings and descriptions. Since poems usually have fewer words than text, every word has to count!

The best way to know more about poetry is to read some! Here are some great titles you can start with. Ask your librarian for more.

1. ***I'm Just No Good at Rhyming: And Other Nonsense*** by Chris Harris: Hilarious pun poems and goofy rhymes that get you giggling. (Ages 5+)

2. ***A Poke in The I*** by Paul Janeczko: Thirty "concrete poems" where the words take surprising shapes on the page. (Ages 6+)

3. ***Dark Emperor and Other Poems of the Night*** by Joyce Sidman: Poems about natural science and nocturnal life in the forest. (Ages 7+)

3 BOOKS
I'd Give as a Present

Think of three people
and a book they each might love.

TITLE: _____
_____

TO: _____

TITLE: _____
_____

TO: _____

TITLE: _____
_____

TO: _____

DECEMBER HIGHLIGHTS
AND FAVORITES!

📖 Book I'd Recommend to My Friends: _____

_____

🌐 A New Place I Read About: _____

_____

😝 Silliest Character: _____

_____

📘 Best Book Cover: _____

_____

🧑‍🏫 Someone Who Read to Me (or With Me): _____

_____

_____

JUST FOR FUN!

Build a fort or tent and read inside it!

Check the Beanstack App to Fill In These Stats:

Longest Book Read:

Number of Reading Sessions:

Most Pages in a Session:

Total Books Read:

You've done amazing things in the last four months, power reader! Go to Beanstack or Beanbright to see all the titles you've read recently—take a look back at those, and fill in some book titles here to complete your personal library.

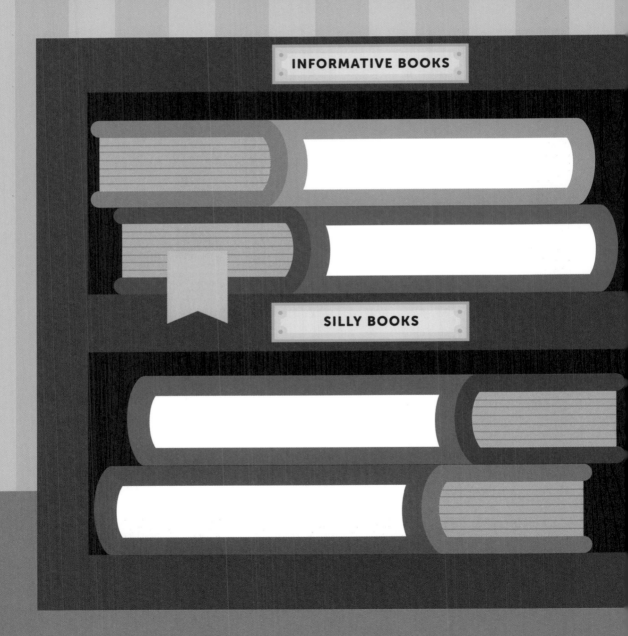

INFORMATIVE BOOKS

SILLY BOOKS

CREATIVE BOOKS

THRILLING BOOKS

END OF FALL AWARDS

Get your sticker
from the back
of the book!

#1

WAY TO GO!

Total Books Read So Far This Year:

_____

Alarm Clock

Apple Picker

Calculator

Crunchy Leaves

Equinox

Hot Cocoa

Leaf Drop

Pumpkins

Reading Ghost

Scared Spider

School Bus

Windy Day

Bamboo Book

Book on Tape

Clay Tablet

Comic Book

Digital Brain

Digital Tablet

Gutenberg Book

Manuscript

Paperback Novel

Papyrus

Scroll

Virtual Reality Glasses

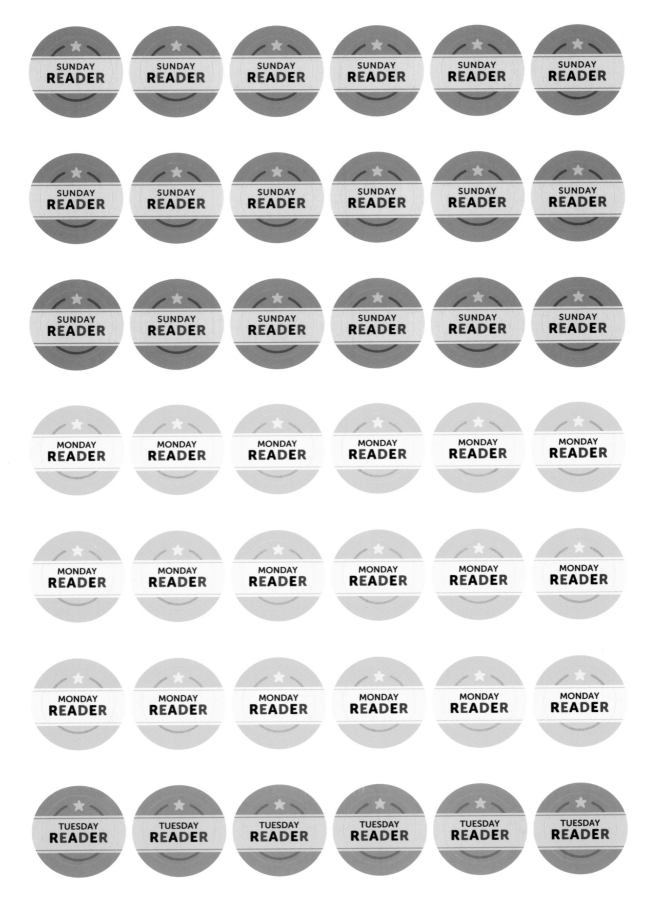

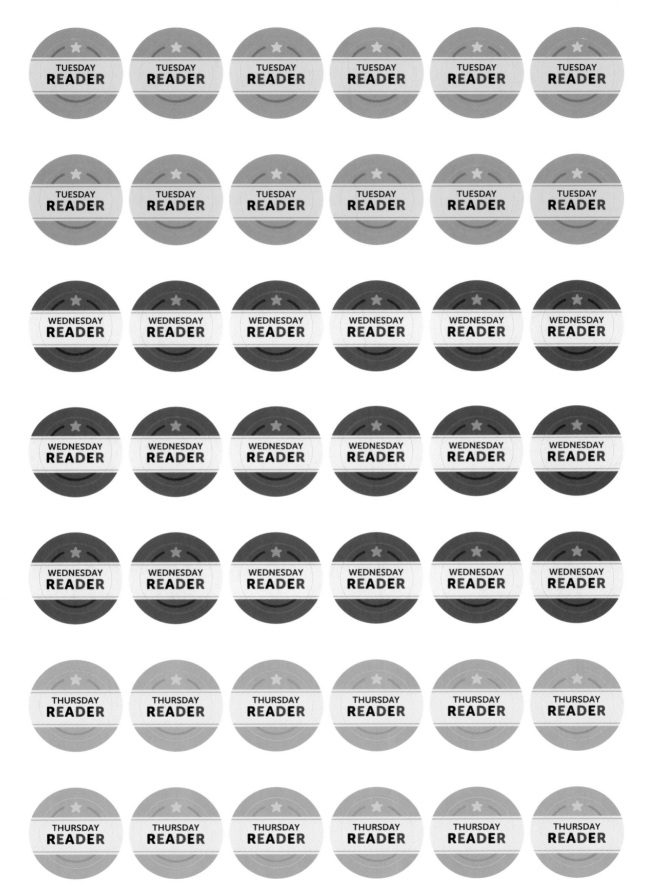

1st Sign-Up Badge

2nd Sign-Up Badge

September
Certificate of Achievement

November
Certificate of Achievement

End of Fall Award

Looking for something new? We recommend these books for a great range of stories, settings, and characters.

FOR AGES 4-7:

- **Camp Tiger** – *Susan Choi*
- **The Scarecrow** – *Beth Ferry*
- **The Thing About Bees** – *Shabazz Larkin*
- **Going Down Home with Daddy** – *Kelly Lyons*
- **Fry Bread: A Native American Family Story** – *Kevin Maillard*
- **Saturday** – *Oge Mora*
- **The Proudest Blue: A Story of Hijab and Family** – *Ibtihaj Muhammad*
- **My Papi Has a Motorcycle** – *Isabel Quintero*
- **Another** – *Christian Robinson*
- **Small in the City** – *Sydney Smith*
- **Planting Stories: The Life of Librarian and Storyteller Pura Belpré** – *Anika Denise*
- **Hey, Water!** – *Antoinette Portis*
- **Crab Cake** – *Andrea Tsurumi*
- **Amy Wu and the Perfect Bao** – *Kat Zhang*
- **Bilal Cooks Daal** – *Aisha Saeed*
- **Freedom Soup** – *Tami Charles*
- **Ojiichan's Gift** – *Chieri Uegaki*
- **When Aidan Became a Brother** – *Kyle Lukoff*
- **Summer** – *Cao Wenxuan*
- **Stormy** – *Guojing*
- **Little Mole's Wish** – *Sang-Keun Kim*
- **Ruby Finds a Worry** – *Tom Percival*
- **Lion of the Sky** – *Laura Salas*
- **Songs in the Shade of the Cashew and Coconut Trees** – *Nathalie Soussana*
- **Where Are You From?** – *Yamile Méndez*
- **Treasure** – *Mireille Messier*
- **Dancing Hands** – *Margarita Engle*
- **It Began with a Page** – *Kyo Maclear*
- **Across the Bay** – *Carlos Aponte*
- **You're Snug With Me** – *Chitra Soundar*

FOR AGES 7-10:

- **What Is Given from the Heart** – *Patricia McKissack*
- **The Bell Rang** – *James Ransome*
- **Soldier for Equality** – *Duncan Tonatiuh*
- **King & Kayla and the Case of Found** – *Fred Dori Butler*
- **Wisp: A Story of Hope** – *Zana Fraillon*
- **Thanku: Poems of Gratitude** – *Miranda Paul*
- **Paper Son: The Inspiring Story of Tyrus Wong, Immigrant and Artist** – *Julie Leung*
- **Todos Iguales: Un Corrido de Lemon Grove**
  All Equal: A Ballad of Lemon Grove – *Christy Hale*
- **Martin & Anne** – *Nancy Churnin*
- **Feed Your Mind: A Story of August Wilson** – *Jen Bryant*
- **Dreamers** – *Yuyi Morales*
- **Up Down Inside Out** – *JooHee Yoon*
- **Little Legends: Exceptional Men in Black History** – *Vashti Harrison*
- **At the Mountain's Base** – *Traci Sorell*
- **What Miss Mitchell Saw** – *Hayley Barrett*
- **Thurgood** – *Jonah Winter*
- **Work It, Girl: Mae Jemison** – *Caroline Moss*
- **The Next President** – *Kate Messner*
- **Stargazing** – *Jen Wang*
- **A Big Bed for Little Snow** – *Grace Lin*
- **The Book Rescuer: How a Mensch from Massachusetts Saved Yiddish Literature for Generations to Come** – *Sue Macy*
- **Carter Reads the Newspaper** – *Deborah Hopkinson*
- **The Wooden Fish** – *Wenxuan Cao*
- **The Kid and the Chameleon** – *Sheri Mabry*
- **Queen of Physics: How Wu Chien Shiung Helped Unlock the Secrets of the Atom** – *Teresa Robeson*
- **When Spring Comes to the DMZ** – *Uk-Bae Lee*
- **Hello, Crochet Friends!** – *Jonah Larson*
- **Just Right: Searching for the Goldilocks Planet** – *Curtis Manley*
- **Magic Ramen: The Story of Momofuku Ando** – *Andrea Wang*
- **Mario and the Hole in the Sky** – *Elizabeth Rusch*
- **Out of This World: The Surreal Art of Leonora Carrington** – *Michelle Markel*
- **Corey's Rock** – *Sita Brahmachari*
- **The Tree and Me** – *Deborah Zemke*
- **Vivaldi** – *Helge Torvund*

Guest Book

Show off your reading! Ask your family, teachers, and friends
to check out your Badge Book, sign your guest log,
and leave a comment. You earned it!

Name:

Comments:

Name:

Comments:

Name:

Comments:

Name:

Comments:

Name:

Comments:

Name:

Comments:

Name:

Comments:

Name:

Comments:

Name:

Comments: